MW00417198

WHAT I HAVE I OFFER WITH TWO HANDS

The Poiema Poetry Series

Poems are windows into worlds; windows into beauty, goodness, and truth; windows into understandings that won't twist themselves into tidy dogmatic statements; windows into experiences. We can do more than merely peer into such windows; with a little effort we can fling open the casements, and leap over the sills into the heart of these worlds. We are also led into familiar places of hurt, confusion, and disappointment, but we arrive in the poet's company. Poetry is a partnership between poet and reader, seeking together to gain something of value—to get at something important.

Ephesians 2:10 says, "We are God's workmanship . . ." *poiema* in Greek—the thing that has been made, the masterpiece, the poem. The Poiema Poetry Series presents the work of gifted poets who take Christian faith seriously, and demonstrate in whose image we have been made through their creativity and craftsmanship.

These poets are recent participants in the ancient tradition of David, Asaph, Isaiah, and John the Revelator. The thread can be followed through the centuries—through the diverse poetic visions of Dante, Bernard of Clairvaux, Donne, Herbert, Milton, Hopkins, Eliot, R. S. Thomas, and Denise Levertov—down to the poet whose work is in your hand. With the selection of this volume you are entering this enduring tradition, and as a reader contributing to it.

—D.S. Martin
Series Editor

What I Have
I Offer With Two Hands

poems

JACOB STRATMAN

CASCADE *Books* · Eugene, Oregon

WHAT I HAVE I OFFER WITH TWO HANDS
Poems

The Poiema Poetry Series

Cascade Books
An Imprint of Wipf and Stock Publishers
199 W. 8th Ave., Suite 3
Eugene, OR 97401

www.wipfandstock.com

PAPERBACK ISBN: 978-1-5326-7745-8
HARDCOVER ISBN: 978-1-5326-7746-5
EBOOK ISBN: 978-1-5326-7747-2

Cataloging-in-Publication data:

Names: Stratman, Jacob

Title: What I have I offer with two hands / Jacob Stratman.

Description: Eugene, OR: Cascade Books, 2019 | Series: Poiema Poetry Series | Includes bibliographical references and index.

Identifiers: ISBN 978-1-5326-7745-8 (paperback) | ISBN 978-1-5326-7746-5 (hardcover) | ISBN 978-1-5326-7747-2 (ebook)

Subjects: LCSH: Poetry. | American poetry—21st century.

Classification: PS94.S77 2019 (print) | PS94 (ebook)

Manufactured in the U.S.A.   OCTOBER 28, 2019

To Benjamin Curtis and Jude Hadley

"Which of you fathers, if your son asks for a fish, will give him a snake instead? Or if he asks for an egg, will give him a scorpion? If you then, though you are evil, know how to give good gifts to your children, how much more will your Father in heaven give the Holy Spirit to those who ask him!"

–LUKE 11:11-13, NIV

"Don't blame me. If they're lies, they're all inherited."

–MY FATHER

Table of Contents

TABLE OF CONTENTS

I. Poems for My Sons

For My Sons at Advent

This will become something. Even though
she implied her suitcase, now empty,
could be, perhaps, used for dirty clothes,
I loved her more for that moment,
for that sentence, for the hope that one thing
could open itself more readily to cease
being itself—to deny itself everything in order
to be another thing, for the spaces

that the pronouns created to invite
anything—the *this*—now to be seen
as, well, anything else—the *something*,
for the patience. First, the declaration,
then the desire to anticipate, to wait
for what *this* will become.

For My Sons on Their First Eucharist

When the bird feeders lay barren
for a few days, as I have forgotten
to buy seeds or your mom wants to rid

the yard of cowbirds and starlings,
and they begin to sway without rhythm
in the summer winds, the mourning doves

come, bound by what they pursue,
uninterrupted, picking lost seeds
among the shells—these gleaners

profiting on the sporadic eating
habits of finches. Forgive me
for not acknowledging the finches

as kind benefactors, the Boaz
of backyard birds. They are not.
They are messy and wasteful,

but we love their colors. Nervously
pecking—like Tolstoy's Vasily
Andreevich, the master in crisis,

the fat man with two coats, groping
for warmth and the horse's reins
in the growing cold and darkness—

the doves don't rest or notice the family
of squirrels running circles or the robin
who lands on the shepherd's hook, surveying

the yard, or the hopeful finches, one or two,
back now, who perch for a moment
and peck at emptiness. These doves

are usually the last to leave
when the cat comes, when I open
the back door, when leftover

seeds are gone. Is constantly searching
for food part of their essence?
Should we pity those made

to search? To be always in want?
Is this mourning? Or is it hope?
Waiting and expecting that seeds

will reappear from above by means
they cannot know, and from below
by a provisional grace?

For My Sons When They Can't Fix It

I broke Joseph's neck, and no amount of good
glue could cover the fine crack there. For guests,
I would point to the three-legged sheep leaning
against the camel or the shepherd holding
the bagpipe, the lost leg long gone from anyone's
memory. I might redirect their attention
toward the chipped wings of the angel propped
piously above the holy family or wonder aloud
with anybody who would listen
why there might be moss on the manger,
in such a dry climate. If desperate, I'd yell
about the damn bagpipes, but the guest, often
as not, inevitably inquired about Joseph's neck,
the forgotten, dismissed, ignored of the story,

standing there in front of the manger, slightly
behind the mother, cracked neck, hands clasped
in prayer, no room for a bouquet of lilies
or spikenard, none that I could find
in mom's cupboard or in the backyard
among the mint and dead asparagus,
none we should crush into an ointment
and ooze into and around the fragments,
nothing to heal these memories:
a child's hands, a family heirloom.
Christ's father now, without doubt
or reservation, despite troubling dreams, waits
to be positioned, hands clasped, head bowed,
crack and all, ready to be loved, to be fixed.

For When My Sons Are Criticized

ending in a thought by Henri Nouwen

I read student evaluations at the end
of the day, walking home
or during a late committee meeting,
like you might read the menu board
at McDonald's, knowing in full
what is in front of you but performing
the obedient act anyway.
But "do not give up or get frustrated"
invites me, interrupts me
to see myself a different animal,
shedding something but not naturally
like the cicada shell or snake skin—
part of the rhythm of a thing. Like watching
my son take off a shirt that is too small,
his head stuck, his ears reddening.

Was this was a violence—a shifting
of a foundation poorly laid? These words
of restoration and wholeness became,
maybe more beautifully, the recognition
that those words, our words, my words cannot
will not be whole, no matter the will or effort,
but that the desire to restore, knowing
that splinters and gaps of knowing will remain
might not be a place of irritation
and frustration but joy
in the mystery of the unknown,
the unknowable. Then we will become
present to each other, not as opponents,
but as those *who share the same
struggle and search for the same truth.*

For My Sons on Transfiguration Sunday, Thinking about School on Monday

with lines from the Companion to the Book of Common Worship

You have always called it your pack-pack,
stuffed with crumpled paper, last week's
notices and permission slips now forgotten,
broken pencils, stripped crayons, a crumb
or four from classroom parties, stuck zippers—
faded characters, superheroes two seasons
too old, straps too loose hanging off your shoulders,
as if it never fit just right. This is all we have:
the old, the used, the broken, the not yet.
I think of you standing on this side of the threshold
a few minutes before you leave for the day
as I read, *It is given us for our journey*
through Lent toward the agony of the cross
and the victory of the empty tomb.
Any interpreter of putting *new wine*
in old skins needs to watch you with care
put your new pencil case in your pack-pack,
navigating the broken zipper with your face
set toward school. You must descend the hill
first from us, from the hug and kiss that we pray
sustain you before you ascend
the other hill. We do not know how much
you carry with you on this walk to school—
even this place with the cross on it,
more your Golgotha than your empty tomb
on some days, on most. *Whose glory shone*
even when confronted with the cross. Please
remember that we are pleased with you,
whose laces rarely stay tied, whose knees
are always skinned and scratched, whose body
shows itself broken each day. Carry this hope

with you through the valley of basketball
courts and playgrounds, between your home
and your school, this hope stuffed
somewhere in your worn pack-pack, between
the books and the afternoon snack, between
the now and the not yet: what is spoken,
what is revealed, what light comes from behind
the clouds surrounding us, your witnesses.

For My Sons When the Day is Too Much or Not Enough

Basket of Peaches. *Joseph Decker. 1885, oil on canvas*

The checker at Wal-Mart this morning
thinks the winter weather's been bi-polar.

Record highs one week, then lows in the 20s.
Our little maple started to bud

in mid-February, she says. A hard freeze
has made it sad now, she says. A local

landscaper, a buddy of mine, I tell
her, knows the trees are tough around here.

They'll be fine, he says. It's not like
we're growing peaches anymore

or nothin', I remind her and leave.
But it's hard considering an Arkansas summer

without peaches, even spotted ones
like Decker gives us, half-dumped, upset

from a bucket—the kind, if we couldn't eat,
we'd use for batting practice; the kind,

not spotted and pocked by disease, the old
ladies would turn into cobbler and the old men

would mix with cranked ice-cream; the kind
that might entice an oriole or two to lounge

on a fence post and maybe talk a bit about
the fickleness of the coming spring weather.

For My Sons When They've Been Dating Someone for Awhile

She brings up ideas of Heaven
over a bowl of tomato soup
and grilled cheese.
I wonder if we get jobs there. If so,
I want to be music, she says.
What instrument do you want to play,
I ask? She does not look down,
but her eyes rest in their sockets,
tired, disappointed.
Sipping the warm soup, she whispers
I want to be music, and in the quiet,
I notice the time,
the empty bowl in front of me,
and the increasing width of the table.

For When My Sons Have
to Account for Themselves

"But Mary, virgin, had no sittings, no chance to pose her piety."
Luci Shaw "Announcement"

I keep telling you, when we catch
you in a lie or hear of your casual

disobediences, that integrity
is doing the right thing when no one

is looking, which is crap, we both know,
or at least I am beginning to smell

its stale bumper sticker odor. Someone
is always watching. You are never alone,

never beyond the reach of the one
who knew you before I knew to consider

you. Never too far above or below
the one who cares for, nurtures, attends

to you. Consider your life a nest,
not a bubble or a glass bowl

or a cage, ornate or rusting. Consider
Mary who knew, always resting

in the assurance that she is known,
that she didn't need to rehearse,

she didn't need to pose, her posture,
her words now an anthology

of gestures, of praise, of automatic
awe and love and yes.

For When My Sons Have a Difficult Time Seeing What is in Front of Them

with lines from the Epic of Gilgamesh

I seem to be
            in the business
lately
        and steadily
of convincing myself   that reading
the right poem
                at the right time
                            in the right light,

or hearing
the one piece
            of advice or writing tip,
or discovering
            the perfect
poet,
        or listening
        to a certain
podcast with the right kind
of poets,
                discussing the right
way
of looking
or looking at,
or the right way
of being
with

or for

        or against

                or in,

will, like alchemy

or osmosis

or divine intervention,

turn everything I touch

into what I have intended

               desired

                       longed for

it to be—

that my voice will begin

to build walls,

a square

          mile foundation

of language,

and then they will come

to *examine*

the brickwork,

they will ask

          how the *bricks were fired*

in the oven, they will walk

back and forth

and wonder:

did the Seven Sages

        not lay its foundations?

If only I could *see*
the Deep
like these
poets

       like these?
if only I could find
the flower

          at the bottom

                  of the sea,

the one promised
to me,
the one

         given
to me in dreams?

The only
assurance

         I seem to rest in
is all I do not have

              and what I cannot claim.

And then you enter, one who should be in bed
at this hour, who hasn't brushed his teeth,
or gone to the bathroom one last time,
who says that he needs just one more strawberry
who needs to tell me one more story;
one who has taken and is taking this moment
from me, my solitude, like the snake,
and gone back to his warm den, and I am left in
the kitchen with dinner's cold dishes
waiting my attention, a blank page
in front of me, and the image of your cowlick,

flattened high on your forehead, white-blond
and always disobedient to the comb's
touch, but beautiful. Can't you see how beautiful?

For My Sons on Ash Wednesday

Our lord of misrule, this five-year-old Falstaff,
after too much root beer and chicken fries,

wearing a Burger King crown and waning
ash-cross on his forehead—only the bottom

of the vertical line now showing itself
below the cardboard edge that slides

down toward the arch of his nose—
wonders aloud why he needs to give

up anything for Lent—why, he should
have to love television, computer games,

juice boxes, even cookies less, then excuses
himself from the table, walks to his room

with his crown now almost covering his eyes,
rests his head on his bed, and whispers in sighs

only the Spirit can hear. *Uneasy
lies the head that wears the crown.*

Uneasily, I lay my head besides his ashes
his dust his waning cross and stained lips,

his growing and groaning body broken
with the weight that is all of him.

For When You Wear Your Crapped-Out Shoes

Misty Moonlight. *Albert Pinkham Ryder. 1885.*
oil on canvas. 11 ¼ x 11 ¾

I think of Ryder's "Misty Moonlight" each time
I reprimand you for trying to jam your feet,
especially the heels, into new shoes

without untying them first. I want you
to preserve them, to save them, for future
wears. Just like you in these subtle rebellions,

Ryder knew what he was doing, breaking
chemical rules, paying little attention to posterity,
mixing oils, I'm told, with alcohol and candlewax

and other types of paint that just don't work well
together over time. He knew better. He paid no mind
to the rules set down before him. And now

his paintings are dying, ruining. But here I stand,
looking at the back of your cracked, wrinkled,
stained shoes as you look at Ryder's barely legible

vision of a sailboat at night, and I love
its life even more, even though (or maybe because)
it fades just slightly each second I take it in.

For When My Sons Grieve with Those Who Grieve

Raspberries in a Wooded Landscape.
William Mason Brown. 1865-1878.

The neighbors brought a small basket
of raspberries to the house yesterday
while you were playing out back.

When their son died three years ago, the oldest
of six boys, they planted a row
of raspberry bushes in the front yard,

where the basketball goal had been
before the storms came. No timely
metaphor here. Supercells come strong

each spring in Arkansas, and the hoop
wasn't well anchored. These berries
do not look as forsaken or lost, though,

as Brown's—his all scattered on the ground,
as if dropped in mourning or fear. These berries
have a redness, a tartness, a seasoned

reminder—a commemoration—
of that which once stood there
in the front yard. We could eat them

on ice-cream or in smoothies
or just one at a time. Yes, we should
eat them one at a time, like stopping

on our walk while a long line of cars
pass, like taking off our hats when we
enter buildings, or like standing

up to greet a stranger. Next time,
when they come, take the small basket
with two hands, boys. Remember, two hands.

For My Sons about Confession

I know I owed our hostess an apology
for accusing her duck mousse pate

of being braunschweiger. I really liked
it. Pop would slab a thick slice on a saltine

with brown mustard. Each time he'd tell us
how his pop would end each meal with a small

glass of sauerkraut juice, sort of like
the port she served that night. I owed her

another apology for drinking
that too quickly. Your uncle says I don't

owe her anything: *tube meat's tube meat
and shots are for shootin*. But it was delicious.

All of it, even the smile she shared
at the door, one you might call polite

but Grandma called a shit-eater.

For When My Sons Think They Need Smartphones

I responded politely, I remember: "No thank you, Ma'am, I don't care for cobbler." This is how my mother taught me to decline food at church pot-lucks and other formal gatherings. As a preacher's kid who found himself at wedding receptions, cake and punch receptions after funerals, and often at different congregants' homes for dinner parties, this piece of advice worked like gold every time I was offered food that I could not pronounce or iden-tify. Usually this was enough to end the conversation and sometimes get a response like, "you're such a polite, young man" or "that's ok, I didn't like it when I was your age, either." This time was different, however. The woman paused, knife in hand, head slightly leaning over the dessert dishes but turned toward me, and said, "But it's peach cobbler. And we also have apple. They both just came out of the oven. I made them. Who doesn't like cob-bler?" I felt my face warming. I said my lines; I knew the script. This wasn't how it was supposed to go; this woman had gone rogue. She didn't tell me that I was polite. She didn't offer me a slice of the chocolate éclair just on the other side of the cobblers. She didn't even smile. Without hesitation, she began cutting a fairly large piece of peach cobbler. The smile that did appear on her face when she handed me the plate would have impressed the Cheshire Cat. Yes, my mother raised a polite boy, but also a boy who could read social clues. Knowing I was beat, I took a piece of the peach cobbler, with a scoop of homemade vanilla ice-cream, said thank you politely, and walked away.

As I returned to my seat at the square card table in the living room, I began to have these faint, wispy memories of summer church potlucks in the country when we lived in Nashville. I remembered fishing in ponds; walking down dry creeks looking for snakes and other confused creek critters searching for water; my mother chasing swans that eventually chased my father, nipping his legs; coleslaw and baked beans; fried chicken and lots of watermelon; the dessert table filled with pies, cakes, and cookies; and, I also remembered my mother pointing to a dish of cobbler, saying, "oh, honey, you wouldn't like that. Grab one of those brownies over there on that paper plate." And, as I sat there at my new girlfriend's home, holding a fork right above my first bite of peach cobbler—one that was basically forced into my hands by my new girlfriend's mother, a woman who was also my former high school English teacher, it became intensely clear to me that my mother had *often* told me at various family get-togethers and church events that I would not like the cobbler and that I should just grab a brownie or a cookie. Even though my memory of those moments can be as thin as the crust on top of that peach cobbler sitting in front of me, I had these fleeting images of my mother returning to the dessert table for a second, maybe even a third, piece of cobbler—that cobbler that she had just warned me against.

As I took my first bite of peach cobbler, with the scoop of homemade vanilla ice-cream, now a 19-year old college student, my world began to shift slightly. It was delicious. That's not the right word. It was everything that I deserved as a flourishing human being. But instead of believing that I had been told a lie my whole life (which I had) or damning my mother to the circle of hell set aside for parents who do not allow their kids to enjoy the sweeter, more luxurious parts of life at any age, I actually began to love and appreciate my mother more—that woman who refused to relinquish a moment of pure goodness and delight to some tow-headed, skin-kneed, snaggle-toothed kid of hers who couldn't appreciate good cobbler.

How much of her life was about sharing, about sacrificing? Instead of sitting in a sudsy tub, sighing, "Calgon, take me away," she chose to stand in the middle of a crowded kitchen, resisting any demand, wish, or question that I had, whispering, "Cobbler, make him go away . . . for just a minute." What did I know I was missing when I ate those cheap, store bought brownies? I'm sure I ate the cookie or the brownie or the Little Debbie snack cake and felt good about myself and ran back out to the creek with my friends to look for snakes and frogs and crawdads. I didn't deserve to eat something taken from a generations-old recipe. It simply wasn't my time for cobbler. My palate wasn't ready for the warm, rich, flaky crust. I wasn't emotionally prepared to appreciate the fruit, picked that season, that week, perhaps, from a nearby orchard. Cobbler might kill a kid. It's just too much tension between cold and hot, crisp and goo. Too much paradox. My mother wasn't denying me one of life's pleasures. She protected me from seeing all other desserts as failures and imposters, from one day saying to my future mother-in-law, "No thanks. I've been eating cobbler my whole life. Got any Oreos?

For My Sons When We Confess Our Sins in Worship

The new pastor has moved the practice of passing
the peace until after we confess our sins
corporately and privately. It did not take an act

of God or even a majority vote from the elders—
just a brief explanation that he found it strange,
difficult, maybe impossible, to extend, to offer,

to invite peace to anybody sitting around us
if we do not have any in our hearts to begin
with. It is symbolic of course, a liturgical gesture

toward a truth we cannot uphold regularly,
exercise graciously, or will into existence. We walk
around the sanctuary, only for a few minutes, mind you,

with our sins stuffed deep in our pockets, fingering them
like snacks we've snuck in, while we shake hands
with the other. Maybe the left hand should know

what the right hand is doing in this instance—a deception
in need of revelation? Maybe we should greet each other,
offer what we have, with two hands, even if one of them

shakes, seems limp, comes in too hard, too firm.
They have come in peace, after all, these hands,
after a washing, even if they need to be convinced.

For My Sons to Read at the End of the Day

Like boys wearing oversized suit jackets
still on hangers, up on the rusting peak
of an abandoned A-framed diner,
the color of blue decades in decay,
a wake of turkey vultures is perched.
None are in flight. None circle above.

They have descended, resting in a row
above the few cars that pass
on this road at the edge of town.
It is too late for tricks, the sun
already setting does not need to be pushed
back any further.
                    Maybe that's what brings
them here to rest awhile, their burnt heads
bowed slightly beneath rigid shoulders,
no gratitude given them for the cool
breezes—fresh this early summer evening—
they urged forth, a grace now extended.

For When My Sons Move out of the House

Looking at William Trost Richards' Landscape *at Crystal Bridges*

Thin clouds in the sliver of sky, tinged
with the green grass it seems to reflect,
announce the day is just beginning
or that night will arrive soon—that we
are at the edge of something.

The shadows, not soft and inviting,
like pillows and blankets, but expanding
like truths we may not desire but welcome,
appear on grassy banks of the stream,
surrounding the light, attentive
and attending, that strikes the little
waterfall, ushering in ripples
from another stream or a bigger pond,
or perhaps the source, below the large rock
covered by the greenness, the fullness,
the abundance of forest.

On one of the banks, the one that leans
closest into the light, under the canopied tree,
I look for my son with his fishing pole
and favorite lure, the plastic crawdad
that wiggles and jerks, depending on the speed
of the reeling, or maybe just a section
of a fat Canadian crawler he's got
scrunched on a gold hook, just resting,
without the reliance of a bobber or slip-weight,
a few yards out from his feet.

I look and look for him looking for smallmouth
or the varieties of pan-fish that lounge
in shade when the sun has just appeared
or is getting ready to depart.

I know not to look for him standing
on the waterfall, knowing the slipperiness
of the green there, too close to risk, and I know
not to look for him beyond the tree line,
in that distant field, peeking between
the trees, too far from the stream,
from the carefully calculated chance
to look at a catch up close, to put his small

thumb inside the small mouth of a bluegill
or speckled sunfish, wanting to put it back
quickly, not to kill it, but to reward
its risk with homecoming.

I look, knowing he is not there—that gap-toothed,
cow-licked boy is not on the bank under that tree,
or any tree, holding the fishing pole, looking
into the shallows of the stream.

But to save us both, I will look.

For My Sons about Grace

"All of my heroes sit up straight." –Gregory Alan Isakov

My son slouches when he walks,
shoulders rounded, chin jutted
forward, moving slow
and savvy like Cecil the Turtle,
outwitting Bugs Bunny at every

turn. If the boy knew to say,
"ain't I a stinka," I bet he would.
In the church he sits, shoulder
blades pinned to the pew, enough
room between the seat and his lower

back to place a small child
or a couple of Eucharist plates.
At the altar of the rollercoaster,
the disembodied voice whispers,
"put your head back against the seat"—

the lap bar requiring our bodies
to obey 90 degrees before
we are launched 65 mph in fewer
than three seconds, and I grin,
my face flattening voluntarily

with glee as my son's back is straight
and his chin parallel with the earth
that is now hundreds of feet below
him, his eyes directed in front—
to seek the next turn or drop or twist

with hope with hope with faith with love,
I hope. He is forced into this position,
yes, I see that, and his shoulders
will curve again as the earth curves,
as the turtle's shell curves, keeping

him safe for now, but he did love
the ride, even how it broke
his wishes, his routine, his desires
and flattened him to its will.
Even then. Especially then.

For When My Sons Yell at God

Jonah Leaving the Whale
Jan Breughel the Elder. Oil on panel (38 x 56 cm) ca. 1600

*"It is a childish work—the whale has the head of a dog
and Jonah looks suspiciously fresh."*
—www.artbible.info

In candied red, the white-bearded
prophet emerges, hands still clasped in prayer,
clean, really clean, maybe too clean, first-day-
of-school clean, baptism clean. Perhaps it is
a childish painting, the punished coming up
for air after a three-day, divine timeout,
begging and pleading inside this flesh
box. Sincere or not, he's out, old and fresh
in a world around him, Breughel is sure
to make clear, swirling blue-black and solid
brown—the earth's bruising, perhaps a wish
of yellow, healing in the distance, a light
faded behind the eye's focus. The dogfish
eyes, big and rolling back. The mouth open

like the cave, like the tomb, like the brown creek
carp we refuse to touch, hate to catch, squishy
and formless but counted nonetheless. But
Jonah will dirty himself again after Nineveh,
under the vine, cussing at God, telling
God His own business, and he will forget
the welcoming red, the fresh fruit color
of that cloak—the thin (or thinning) clearing
in the background beyond sea and storm,
even the mouth as exit, as release.
He will soon forget to consider how
suspicious it is for a man like him
sitting in death's darkness for three days
to come out so clean, so bright, so forgiven.

When You Walk Off to School in the Morning

"What lives beside us passing for air?"
from "Life on Mars" by Tracy K Smith

Is it joy or hubris that carries you
out the door each morning assuming
you'll return? Is unthinking a kind
of freedom? Does your brother have reason
for fear or doubt—shouting to your mother,
"I hope you'll pick me up today?
Has he tapped into a truth I cannot open,
one that you haven't thought to think about?

What lives beside us passing for air?
Maybe what prompted Philip to visit
the Ethiopian. Maybe what led him
to tease out truth. Maybe what allows you
to come back each afternoon, even after
you march out and away each morning,
arms locked in your pockets, eyes always
forward. Maybe what invites your brother
to giggle in the backseat for what
I have not witnessed. Maybe what saves all
of us from saying the thing we believe
can shade or flavor every other time
we remain still in each other's spaces.

Whatever I want to name it, it is not
of my construction. Whatever I will
it to be or desire it to have, I cannot
own it. I want him to have your air,
yes, but he will be ready for the next
disaster. He is living his smile
and awakened eyes to the constant
of the inconstant, but he is prepared—
he is anchored in the unknown.

It is cold this morning. Wet. The green
leaves are slipping. The brown lawns are settling
into their long rest. And you are taller
than you were when you went to bed last night.

For When My Sons' Marriages Struggle

Reading the sign next to William Trost Richards'
Along the Shore *at Crystal Bridges*

On our honeymoon, drinking
red wine, eating fudge, and riding rusty
beach cruisers on Mackinac Island,

we drove north to Lake Superior
through miles of pine to a state forest
for a long hike, a longer argument,

and bad spaghetti. When we arrived
at Whitefish Point, we parked by the sign
that marked this water as treacherous

for passing ships—the *Edmund Fitzgerald,*
the *Vienna of Cleveland,* the *Comet,*
and the *Cyprus*—now wrecked below.

We could not see them, nor did we desire
to take in their change, their rust, their silence.
We were certain they were beautiful

on a sunny day during their maiden
voyages. If not beautiful, you added, they knew
their job, their purpose. It was a day when clouds

were the same dark as the water—
where there were no boats or people
or birds. Not even birds. Just the dark water,

only briefly turning white, long enough
to "crash violently against the shoreline."
The lighthouse behind us, long ago turned

into a shipwreck museum, welcoming visitors
and experienced divers, remained closed that day.
We stood there, as we do now, miles from the bed

and breakfast, yards away from the shoreline,
a body-length apart from each other, staring out
to the horizon, praying for the sun to break through.

For When My Sons Pray

"Language supplies us with ways to express ever subtler levels of meaning, but does that imply that language gives meaning, or robs us of it when we are at a loss to name things?" –Lucy Greely's Autobiography of a Face

I hand feed my fire-eel, a dinner-guest,
like me, announced. So not to reveal
my ignorance and confusion so readily,

I stared at the salt-water tank,
just over and beyond her left shoulder,
hoping for a clue—for the image

to appear, there among the little
blue nameless fish and the pink, speckled,
plastic rocks. *Never have I heard*

that sentence before, I spoke to the guest
next to me, mystery growing inside
me, as one who hears a foreign tongue

for the first time or the new believer
trying to mouth along with the other congregants
as they recite together the Apostle's Creed

or the Lord's Prayer. No one or thing
in that farmhouse in the Northeast corner
of Oklahoma could help me: not the woman's

face, not her hand gestures, while she described
the process, not the fish tank behind her.
Now, I notice young men and women hold

their hands out, elbows still touching their hips,
with palms empty, facing up, while they pray,
while they search for (are witness to) meaning.

When the woman Googled *fire eel* and passed
her phone around the table so that we could all see
and believe, I knew then, with my hands open,

face up, hidden on my lap, one hand now holding
the phone, the picture, the fire eel, true and awful,
that God could not exist for those at this table.

For When My Sons Fight With the Ones They Love

I know a guy
who had a sextuple bypass

yesterday. Forgiveness
is nearly impossible

for the human heart,
without such issues,

this weakened muscle
with its cracks

and fissures, its plaque
build-up, narrowing

any space for blood
flow, its irregularity,

its want to beat
too fast or too slow,

its mirrors
that reflect images

larger, closer than they actually appear,
its bruises that rarely

turn yellow. This is not
a poem. This is a plea.

For My Sons after a Tornado Warning

To help, I wish my parents would have assured
me that the late afternoon, on-coming squall
line was simply the night sky, a tarp,
surely, unrolling from the west southwest—
orchestrated by a forgotten, younger

brother of Eos. And, if they knew anything
about the one that Zeus feared, they would've
kept her hidden in her cave. I wished to see
their fingers tracing the front of the storm,
narrating its arrival: a blanket, a comfort,

a drape over the humid day. It is true
that I would have believed them in fact,
not questioning the disappearance
of the stars or the thunder
or the flashes in the not so distant

distance. It was the story I wanted—
the night coming to meet me at the end
of each day like the lid I put over
my toy box, the GI Joes and He-Men,
keeping them safe and orderly.

Now, each fall and spring, here
in tornado alley, I am tempted
to tell you, when the birdsongs
of the backyard still, the siren
blasts, the colors of the sky

grow orange and green, and the blackness
of the southwestern horizon,
up from the flats of Oklahoma,
grow large, that it is not Nyx,
the shadowy one, but that silly

little brother of Eos, not really rosy-
fingered or robed in flowers, but riding
a rusty bike carried by two black
Labradors—lapping tongues, wagging
tails, and pink paws, ready to leap

to our chests in greeting, coming now
in a hurry to tuck us all in for the night
and lick our faces and lie next to us
until we wake up, even if tonight
we sleep in the windowless

walk-in closet in the bedroom
at the northeast part of the house,
with our shoes, a few bike helmets,
and a change of old clothes stuffed
discretely in the dark corner, just in case.

For My Sons on the First Day of High School

Standing in front of William Sidney Mount's
Fruit Piece: Apples on Tin Cups *at Crystal Bridges*

It is a still-life, the sign tells me.
Life in stillness.
Life quietly.
It is an apple.
No advertisement
featuring a movie star or pop singer.
No warning
label or nutritional guide.
No marketing
campaign to improve
its consumer rating—
I am looking at you
pomegranate and clementine.
They are apples on tin cups.

In a moment of desperation,
I plead with my students
not to Google
poetry explanations
for their analysis assignment.
I beg them to sit with the poem
—to sit in silence, to be
still
with the poem—
to struggle, I say.
I want you
to enjoy
the struggle, the stillness
without an exact,
immediate answer.

I wonder if what
they need, if what I need, if
what you need,
is to stand for minutes
upon minutes upon minutes
in front of William Sidney Mount's
Fruit Piece" Apples on Tin Cups
and wonder about the apples,
still, on tin.

For When My Sons Expect Too Much From Their Sons

While shooting on goal, at soccer practice,
working on proper form, my son, not keeping
his head and chest over the ball, with plant
foot too far from the ball and his back
as straight as the path to my frustration,
sends it sailing five feet over the crossbar
and another five feet over the ten-foot fence,
with its extra foot of barbed wire. The other boys
freeze as the ball lands in high weeds—
a twenty-yard mote of wildness:
brush and trees, home for snakes, tics, and chiggers.
These boys, professors' and immigrants' sons,
watch the only farm boy
disappear into that place they'd never choose
to go. When my son turns away from the fence
to find another ball, I wonder if he would
ever lie to save a friend, take a beating
to protect a stranger, give his love
a jacket in the rain or cold, clean up
a messy room that isn't his mess to clean,
take care of a blown-out diaper, kneel down
and shovel vomit out of the car, or maybe
even care for his wife's scars from a C-section
that brings the world a boy—a boy that shanks
a ball over a fence and watches
another wade through danger to get it.

For When My Sons Are 43

Scooping my sons' toys from the bath tonight, I notice
Batman's only got a four-pack. Upper abs and obliques,
tight and sculpted. But his thick gold belt with covert
tools covers his lower abs. I get it, Bruce. You're a bit older
than I am, and even though I haven't pulled my brown belt
quite that high getting ready for work, I notice my bath towel
creep up a little each year, and, in the car, I pull the gray
seatbelt, over those abs, just in case my wife gives
my tummy a glance. I don't fight much crime,
but I swim a thousand meters three times a week,
run four or five miles in the dark, and begin the day
with planks and prayer. Yet, if I had that gold, a thick belt
like yours, Bruce, I wouldn't have to suck it in all the time.

For When My Sons Are Bored

Standing in front of Kent House *by Andrew Wyeth at Crystal Bridges*

A house on rocks, the same color
as the rock. Vanilla—muted vanilla.
The door, near the middle
of the painting, is blue. I see
no birch trees for swinging—
not on this shoreline in Maine,
anyway. There is no hawk anywhere
I can see, *motionless in dying*
vision before it knows it will accept
the mortal limit. There is only the rock,
mostly, and the house, similar in color,
and the door—the blue door

the same color as the sky.
You may live in the house
on all of that rock. You may
watch all the TV you wish
or stream movies on your phone
in that house on all of that rock.
You may ignore the windows
and indulge in mirrors. You may argue
whether the kitchen or the bathrooms
are the most important rooms
for profitable resale. You may.
Remember, though, the door leads to the sky.

For When My Sons Enter the Job Market

Don't underestimate the pain
of a black eye. I charge the ball,
chopper hit right to me, knowing

how high bounce leads to a smaller
bounce—a halfy on its way right
into my glove. But this is my first

time on a grass infield, and I misjudge
the lip. A week later, I overestimate
the courage to get into the batter's box.

Just step in there, the coach on first rattles
at me between tobacco spits, staining the dust
between his feet. His meaty index fingers

jab his temples, as he speaks like one who knows.
Think, boy. Think now. And choke up.
The pointers change into fists, one on top

of the other, twisting back and forth,
reducing the imaginary bat handle to dust.
I can only see out of one eye, but I can see love.

He, who comes to practices often with bloody
knuckles and beer breath, knows my limitations.
Choke up. Get low. Think, boy. But he knows

that I am fast and love dirt. *Get on first,
then make them hurt*, is what I hear
as my shoulders relax and my hips

begin to twist, pointing directly toward the ball
released: the direct line of my healing.

45

For When My Sons Mow the Lawn

ending with a line from Joy Kogawa

As I mow the spring weeds, mixing with tufts
of grass, thinking the long thoughts one thinks

during tedious tasks, my memory saves me
as I notice a little patch of dead grass

a few feet ahead, near the half-dead weeping willow
you like to climb. This hand-me down

memory clarifies what's just beyond the dulled blades.
I wasn't very old when I began mowing lawns,

when my mother told me how she ran over a rabbit's
nest—high-pitched screams, too painful to hear,

bone-twigs breaking and blood—and my father
pained and pinned against his lot, grabbed

the merciful shovel in the garage. I stop
the mower and call you from the house

to crouch low and quietly, several feet
from the nest. You watch the dead grass move

with the life that it hides. I cannot help
but cry a little—the mercy I've been given,

the mercy that I see my father hold, the weight
land upon the seed-sized skulls in that nest

on that day, next to my mother still
holding onto the mower, holding on

to the essential thing about truth telling:
do not speak until you come to a place of love.

For My Sons this Sunday Morning

I didn't want his encouragement,
calling my name after each cross-court
backhand, after each solid volley at the net,
after each unforced error, his eyes
on me with each point won and lost.

I didn't want my father to attend
any of my matches, watching my racquet
not fall far back enough on my serve,
my elbow not snap upward, cueing
the wrist into action, my eyes
not lifted high enough to see the ball
in subtle rotation, my shoulders,
my hips not square, not purposeful,
my follow-through not follow through,
not end as it should end, as designed—
all he taught me to avoid, to work against.

Yet, I saw him beyond the parking lot
at the edge of a small green space
next to the road, half-veiled behind a tree
for two hours while I played and pretended
he wasn't there, that I was right,
that I was in this alone, that his presence,
his disobedience, was not love.

For My Sons on Christ the King Sunday

The Doubting Thomas. *Carl Heinrich Bloch. 1882*

In these paintings, like Caravaggio,
for instance, where doubt is erased,

Thomas leans, almost crouches low enough
to see inside the wound, his finger stuffed

there far enough, even to the knuckle,
in want to dam his incredulity.

Take Bloch's Thomas, though, the crouch turned
to kneel, hands up close to his averted

eyes still not seeing Christ's chest bare and slight
glow around his hair, the white robe and shadowed

onlookers. These are not the surprised
hands of Rembrandt. Here Thomas hides,

but his red cloak draws my eyes even
as I try to focus on the cut, the blood

on the one who has returned refined.
When Thomas' hands come down and rest

on his knees, and he allows his eyes to rise
to meet the meat of his undoing, I don't think

he will poke it. I don't think this Thomas
will need to move at all, but he will choose

to rest, stay kneeling, and maybe allow
his eyes back down toward his hands

now not clinched or stiff straight but clasped
loosely like he was taught before bedtime.

II. Poems for Everyone Else, Including My Sons

An Advent Prayer at Springtime

Romans 8: 24-25

When the rose-breasted grosbeaks arrive
with their bleeding hearts at the end
of each April, perch on top of the shepherd's
hook that holds the feeder—their soft song
waking us to spring, there above the chaos
of finches and sparrows, and leave a week
or two later, to summer further north—
do not despair their leaving; do not curse
their departure or the blandness of the brown
female house finches or the couple of mourning
doves that show up each morning in their absence.
Do not wish for their return, as if they may not,
as if your pouting or squinting eyes and pursed
lips will secure their coming back, as if you are
not a child of the miracles of expectation,
of rhythm, of anticipating patience. We do not wish.
We wait. And it will come then that you will be
standing in the kitchen in front of the bay
window on a late April day when the rose-breasted
grosbeaks, again, with their bleeding hearts,
will perch on top of the shepherd's hook
that holds the feeder—their soft song waking
us to spring—there above the chaos of the finches
and sparrows before they leave a week or two
later to summer further north. So be it.

The Juncos Want for Nothing

A family of dark-eyed
juncos have now arrived
at the oak tree feeder.

I say family loosely;
I've only seen the males
scratching the oddly warm

mid-February ground,
never with much interest
in the feeders above:

house finches, goldfinches,
and the bullying house
sparrows. Food will be there,

they think, especially
when my son throws handfuls
of thistle seed around

the base of the feeders.
It's easy to watch them
want for nothing, gleaning

leftovers from the ones
who dance and dive around
each other—acrobats

and pugilists, grabbing
the easy spot to eat,
letting only a few

seeds drop. Juncos are blind
to accidental grace,
never acknowledging

their benefactors—just
here, scratching and bowing.
I'm watching the juncos,

reading family texts
about your surgery,
while reaching for a light

thread, the metaphor's deft
linchpin. It evades me,
mostly, swaying somewhere

above my head, while I,
face down, want for everything
and write nourishing lines.

A Poem for My Wife, Sitting at the Computer Thinking About Our Sons

Saint Nicholas Saves Three Innocents from Death
(1888) by Ilya Repin

1.
The blade is not parallel with the land—
brown, flat, and obscured by all the bodies
crowding around the spectacle, almost
the same color as the foggy, blurred sky
and barely visible mountains. St. Nick's right
hand holds the sword at the hilt, his left
approaches and reproaches death's sentence,
and the child, in the back of the crowd,
hand on his head in his white shirt, the same
shade as the sky, as the savior's stole, waits.

2.
According to Repin, he looks blind,
so fastened to the truth, like a seer,
like Tiresias burdened by light;
his gaze far off away from this violence;
the sword and bare neck, this horror
on the faces of the old man and fellow
innocents that he cannot bear to bring
his eyes down on the silent steel, thick
shining and central here, the executioner,
the saved men in their women's clothing,
it seems, their looted goods, as the story
goes, their mistakes, missteps, bare chests
bared for answers, bared for saving.

3.

I hate to write; I like to watch you
sit at the computer reading stories
about St. Nicholas, how he calmed
the storm as he journeyed to the Holy Land,
how he saved a man from prostituting
his daughters by throwing gold pieces
through the window and running away
into the shadows, about his penchant
for anonymity, his penchant to save
to stave the sword meant for the innocent.

4.

It is late September. The heat broke
only yesterday, and you are already
in preparation, waiting for the prescribed
time for the calendar to say that it's time
to wait, but you are already there
in love in anticipation in your head,
filling their shoes with oranges and gold
chocolate coins, filling their memories,
finding the right story to right their hearts,
to mend the gaps and fissures, waiting
for the baby born even as you see
the sword always in the shadows, always
swinging above their heads tied, you hope,
you pray by rope so thick the sword is only
metaphor, only reminder, only dream.

The Weavers

Remember the punch-line from the family
story we always told at Christmas; the one
that forced us to the internet to learn more

about the Moravians, more than the spice
and sugar cookies we would eat, thin as our memory
of them; about Jan Hus a Lutheran before Luther,

tried and condemned at the Council of Constance
standing straight and solemn in black cloak,
according to Brozik in the middle of the painting,

in the middle of accusing color and gaze,
later to be burned for heresy; the story
that brought Tom to mind, the kind church

sexton who couldn't see well,
who played in a bowling league, ate apples whole—
core and all—and let us pull the bell ropes

to welcome the chosen frozen; the story
that always led to more talk about nativity
scenes, the kind that use live animals,

the ones outside McDonalds that use
the Hamburgler, Ronald, and the Fry Guys
as the holy family, or the more dramatic ones

that use live plants mosses stones sticks
and little mirrors for water to show Christ's
birth ministry death; the story that left Mom in tears;

the one that needs to be woven each year
while we wait for childhood to return
like the winter cedar waxwings

decorating tree tops with red and gold,
those holidays of hyperbole woven
in the early hours of day carefully

like Grandma rising early to make bread
or Hayden's father shining shoes in the dark—
a preparation, a commemoration, a eulogy,

a liturgy; the story in waiting, unwoven
only to be retold, rewoven, renewed
the next year with bolder strokes, brighter colors?

A Poem I Give to my Sons My Father Gave to Me

Who watches me? Who stands a good distance
from where I stand, on a hill, perhaps, looking
down at my shoulders; who knows more than I;
who sees further, deeper; who waits longer;
who rests in the flurry of feelings?

I want to know what he knows, to forget
what he forgets, to sense what he senses,
to recognize, interpret, and signal
what he can, while he watches me watching
you watch these kids play their reindeer
games without you. To behold is to absorb
the pain and the longing. To see is to love.

Ubi amor, ibi oculus,
or is it Ubi oculus, ibi amor?

Watching Mark Twain's *Is He Dead?* With My Son

We know the punch-line is coming. The tension here in Act 2
is predictably drawing to a sweet, amicable, knee-slapping
conclusion, but we are polite and knowing, having read
Shakespeare and seen episodes of MASH, but still waiting to see
how these kids—actors, make-up and costume-deep in comic
sincerity—will help us rest statically in our expectations.
Not my son, though, this boy, next to me, dressed in a collared shirt
and slacks, prerequisites for a night out together at the theater.
Unlike in church, so immersed and stunned during the first act,
like a raccoon or armadillo in wide oncoming brights,
he leans just a little too far forward into the homespun
dramatic irony and finds himself standing, like sleep walking,
and has to be led back down to sitting. Now that the punch-line
has been delivered, he laughs and laughs, red faced and not breathing
well, and claps, not in applause, confined to decorum, but in praise.
Cupped, hands clap as an echo claps, as response, as reaction
as being led, like standing. And, the adults begin to applaud,
not clap, but I smile knowing that he has led all of us
to this place. Later that evening, I read Updike say
about Winslow Homer that "in his vast space he has his space,
and no more," so I will try, for this moment, to forget
about travel bans and alternative facts, about the enemy
of the enemy of the people, and write these lines that snap
some whip in me—that send, that lead, that propel me to his room
where I kneel in his space to watch him, a calm echo, in breathy sleep.

The Painter

Zeuxis Selecting Models for Helen of Troy. *Angelica Kauffmann,*
1764 and Zeuxis et les Filles de Crotone. *François-André Vincent, 1789.*

Pliny the Elder in *The Natural History* tells
the story of Zeuxis, the painter: In order
to construct beauty—to paint a heaven-size Helen,

not the laughable old Aphrodite, "he had the young
maidens of Crotona stripped for close examination.
He selected five of them in order to adopt

their various parts and pieces for his picture, seeking
the most commendable points in the form of each."
According to Lennard Davis, disability

studies scholar, "the central point here is
that in a culture with an ideal form of the body,
all members of the population are below

the ideal. No one young lady of Crotona can
be the ideal. By definition, one can never
have an ideal body." Davis suggests, then, that we,

always the object, should feel good about this story.
No one can be Helen of Troy. Ok. Fine. But someone
needs to tell that devastated woman in white

at the bottom of Francois-Andre Vincent's version—
one of the many women whose parts, any parts, were not
chosen to be a part of the ideal. Not even

her wrist or ankle. Not the gold of her hair or the nape
of her neck. Not even her Roman nose, now tucked
in the bosom of the woman holding her up.

Is she being told what Pliny the Elder reminds
us: Zeuxis was rich. Way rich. So, "in a spirit
of ostentation, he went so far as to parade

himself at Olympia with his name embroidered
on the checked pattern of his garments in letters of gold."
Maybe that woman, that maid or mother, is whispering,

"you can't trust an ass who parades himself on the street
with his own name on his clothes to have good judgement
about beauty. Oh dear," she might be saying, "if only

time had been kinder to you, to have you born just two
decades earlier, to have known the wit of Angelica
Kaufmann. You could have been the one, not the one in white,

so compliant, complacent, posing in that position you think
you wish for now. Not that one, but the one in red
who slips behind Zeuxis and grabs the brush, in front

of the vast canvas, ready, only briefly looking behind
before beginning, to paint yourself, to construct your self
and not slouching here on my shoulder crying

over that man who would tell Helen to her face
that she should just relax and smile more."

Cedar Waxwings

A family of cedar waxwings have gathered
in the large, bare oak in the corner
of the town cemetery. Like the scratchy
hesitancy of a needle on wax or my son's attempt
at whistling through a mouth of missing teeth,
their song turns in choir with the wind, low but sharp
this morning. Speckled high in the branches,
yards above the gray stones under the tree,
plotted years before sidewalks and wider, paved
streets, their dawn-tipped tails and blood-tipped
wings move in choir with the sun, not yet high
enough to dominate the day, but these bandits
of winter, poised here in mid-March still,
call me to stillness, invite me to pause here,
next to the oak, under their elongated liturgy,
a little longer now, just a little bit longer.

Tennessee Moon

Today was hot. This early
evening, it is difficult
to tell the difference
between the hums
of cicadas
in the trees
from the AC units
on the sides of houses.
We are outside still,
darkness growing
over the backyard.
Punished again.
No *Dukes of Hazzard*
for us, again. Barefoot
and shirtless, we chase
fireflies with big red
plastic bats, leaving the glass
jar on the backporch steps.
We climb the fence
and eat too many cherries
from the neighbor's tree,
and I stab myself,
accidentally,
in the leg with a rusty
Boy Scout knife,
running after the neighbor-boy's
cat, blade out, pointed down,
away from my face
and the Tennessee moon,
big and bright,
now waxing.

Poverty of Heart Makes a Good Host

ending with a thought by Nouwen

The staid and staying notion
that we are always
in the act of becoming,
something I heard
by those older and wiser,
comforts: to know that you do not
know and that you may not know
all you think you ought to
know but that there will be space
to grow and expand and move within the grace
given.
            But then you get married and two
of you are becoming at once, changing
lanes, shifting preferences, moving in various
opposing and crossing directions
and attitudes, like two toddlers
in the same room playing
not together but immersed
in your own selves only sensing
the warmth of another
body nearby.
            But then you have kids,
maybe, and all are becoming
this sanctified and sanctifying
side show, this hall of mirrors where
you cannot see to see each other
becoming, merely gazing at each other
in this vertically horizontally convex
concave maze that distorts, never straightens.

Yet you will remember everything
you love in flux, like caterpillars
that crawl all over your shoulder,

your wrist, your knee
under the oak out back, becoming
the butterflies you chase in hopes
they will rest on your nose,
close now to see love: *the one*
who believes that his guest
is carrying a promise he wants to reveal
to anyone who shows interest.

Bullet Holes in the Arkansas State Sign on the Missouri Border Just South of Noel

I want to believe that she left him one
night, sitting there alone at the Red Barn,
after a couple six or seven beers,

for some lanky Razorback, some kid
with Hog stickers all over his truck.
She just grew tired of tagging along

with an Elk River outfitter—a man content
with the lonely crags and hollows of himself.
I can see him, drunk but steady, under

an owl moon, winds slight from the southwest,
standing on the shoulder of Highway 59,
next to the Hillbilly State Line Liquor Store,

under that large man-sign, with its muscles
and tattered overalls, the hill hat,
the moonshine in one hand and the buxom

blonde in the other, in the only light
for a good stretch, next to the gas pumps,
with the Sig Sauer P225 she bought

him last Christmas, now pointed at the "k"
with his sights set on "a" and "n", knowing
feral hogs are invasive pests.

A Theologian Questions the Boy in George Inness' Landscape with Fisherman

After hearing Mirolsav Volf speak

From where does the light come? Does it begin
behind and above, residing in the liturgical

clouds? Was the light there on the spot
where you sit before you arrived, on the grass

near the stream's banks, calling you
to respond? Do you still call out to God?

Have you asked where he is? Have you asked
why he is hiding? Are you deaf to the call

of transcendence? Do those clouds not command
you to listen? Do you know that you are

a red insignificance at the river's bend?
Do you care? Can you can be in paradise

and still not flourish? Are you continually
in the business of turning stones into bread?

Bread into stones? Is your chief temptation
now your chief end? Are you in wait for something

or someone? To whom are you responsible?
What happens when you fail? Is this your Sabbath?

Are you content? Have you found your space
where you do not need to strive?

On Stillness

DeScott Evans. Daisies, ca. 1885. Oil on linen, 12 x 10⅛ inches.

Storms come hard here, thin and slow, or fat
and slow, rarely fast. Several states long or wide,
they don't travel like freight trains, but like the future,
predictable and inevitable. Pounding rusted, bent nails
flat on loose boards, weakened by straight winds, I notice
the dark knots and think of your daisies inside
a half-filled pitcher hanging on a nail, the sun behind you
setting lone and relieved not to be among wall clouds
and hail storms. Knowing what I know about east-bound
storms and winds that loosen nails decades set still, I hope
you took this jar of flowers down after you finished
painting, you, slightly younger than I am now, taking spare
minutes, like me, away from your children, to attend
to a handful of daisies in a glass pitcher, hanging on a nail
on a wood plank—the next storm beyond your vision.

A Poem I Give to my Son My Mother Gave to Me

Make sure the bag opens with the wind.
Don't try to fight. You'll lose. Place the bag
flat on the edge of the pile, your heels firmly
inside it so it won't fly away. Now,
crouch down over the leaves. With your right
hand, hold the bag; now use the left to shove
the leaves through your legs. I'll rake the rest closer
while you start shoveling. Always keep a rake
close in case there is no one else
around you to help. No, I won't just hold
the bag so you can bring me an armful.
Listen to the wind. What if I'm not
around to hold the bag for you?
What if I'm not able to hold the rake
while you bag the leaves? Make sure to keep
the rake here, next to your feet, right next
to the leaf pile. What if no one is around
to help you? Promise me. Let's get to work.
It's cold. The wind hurts. I'm tired. Place
your heels where I showed you. Crouch down
and start shoveling. I'll rake the pile closer.

When the Lady at the Bank Asks if I Got Stuck Babysitting Today

Has she met the old woman who asked why
I wasn't at work, one morning at the park with you?
Or has she talked with your doctor who praised
my diaper skills and swift swaddling techniques?
Or maybe the wife of a colleague who questioned
my work ethic when she saw me barreling
through the store one morning? Or, yet,
the young women fawning over my goodness
as you sleep, tucked in snug like Roo
in the BabyBjorn? I'm not looking for nods
or their ginger-dipped smiles. I'm looking
for my keys and the grocery list I swear
I must have left on the microwave.

Joy Curves

A Golden Shovel for Marilyn Nelson

Happiness, theologians tell me, is not joy,
but they haven't seen how the ball curves
as it leaves your small hand and begins in
its journey toward my hand—not quite a
straight line, yet still its own trajectory.

Teaching Stigma

I ask students to consider three things
they do not like about themselves,

aspects they hide in the shade
of what they want others to see.

I write my confessions on the board;
they crinkle their noses, bunch

their brows, trying to rid their faces
of discomfort. After minutes of harmless

reflection, of ice-breaking artifice,
I ask them to circle the worst words,

the most problematic in certain
social circles—ones they could wish

away if they gave it language,
a space to grow and then leave.

Then, we go around the room pronouncing
and professing each one: *I'm bad at cooking,*

I'm no good with names, Math.
When I weild a Sharpee and declare to write

that self-selected blemish on their foreheads
so every conversation, every glance,

every question, every indifferent shrug
of the shoulders, every movement in the opposite

direction, and every stare will help that part
of them, that sliver of their existence, that corner

of a shadow, now public, grow big and stale
and become their whole, their constant

and complete, one of them asks if he can choose,
now that he knows, what will be written, and where.

Poem for my 43rd Birthday

After Charles Bukowski's poem of the same name

To end up alone
in the donut drive-thru
retrieving my sons'
chocolate-covered,
the glazed with sprinkles,
the blueberry cake
for their mother
and glad to be there.
And maybe
they're all there too,
the truckdrivers,
third-shifters,
teachers, electricians,
lawyers, everyone
on Bukowski's list
and possibly
more coming in from
or going out into,
waiting nonetheless,
for their whatever
hole it might fill.
And I pull
into the lot,
sun rising,
into my eyes
when I enter,
on my back
when I leave,
on these donuts
at home when,
we all slouch
around the table
ready to receive.

Preacher's Wife Votes for Hillary Clinton

Before the third baseman
for the High Street Baptist Church
co-ed softball team shouted,
Easy out, like it was gospel truth,
and she choked up on the bat
with her mad-as-hell mom hands
and laid down a seein'-eye
single between third and short,
I never saw my mother get mad
at anyone other than my brother
and me—never had I heard her yell
Up yours and give the three-finger salute
to a perfectly good Baptist
in gray coaching shorts.

Down Holly, Right on Granite

Trees around here, this time of year, don't catch
on fire much when the sun hits the leaves;
they just show off their rust a little more.
The oak in the corner of the doctor's
parking lot, shading the sidewalk as I pass,
balds quickly, hanging hard onto the lower
leaves after first freeze—the street drain clogged
now until Christmas. At the turn, I find
a quarter and kick it to defraud
any trick—string or glue—then hand it over
to my son at home, magic still caught
in air around him, and watch him wonder
about quarters appearing on his street—
watch him ignite with possibilities.

The Tufted Titmouse

For Marquita

No finches again today at the feeder;
the squirrels are acrobatic and relentless.

The tufted titmouse, with its blue-gray
bedhead, new to the area, scouts

from places beyond my view—grabbing
one seed at a time, eating elsewhere,

fleeting, flitty, twitchy, temporary,
off in a tree, a wire, or the next house.

I'm told that my little feeder here
in the corner of Arkansas is helping

you expand your range, your reach, a bit.
It's tough to be new in town, I know,

not sure how long to stay in one spot,
not sure it's a good idea to eat

the food where you find it. Where does
your fear reside—how far deep inside

your making? Are you constantly at a loss
of what to do next? Of where to go?

Are you tired of playing it straight?
Do you look for other feeders

when you're not here? May you rest,
many seeds at once, perched here next

to sparrows, finches, cardinals,
and maybe the rose-breasted grosbeak

when he arrives in April. What little
you see is yours, although little.

Writing a Poem While Listening to a Lecture of *Christ our Paedogogus*

For P.K.

You should know that I saw the plate
of cookies that you baked for your students.

The door was open; they were on the chair.
After making copies, I wandered there

and saw the cookies were in the same place
where you often set goodies that you make.

Weren't they the soft, oatmeal German cookies
from your pilgrim years there, learning the food

and the language? The cookies: bits of fruit
stuck where chocolate is supposed to sit.

I'm writing this note, because I want you
to know that I was overcome by virtue.

An Image after a Student Asks Me if Vocation is only for the Middle Class

I've only ever seen   one squirrel   fully relaxed,
not the constant fidget   of head and forefeet,

of tense muscles   anticipating everything else's
movements, always responding   and reacting,

not enough down time   to put on weight, or to wonder
about trees, leaves, sunshine, or raindrops.   This one

was gray and fat,   climbing up out of a Monday
morning trash can   on the edge of campus, caressing

an unopened Snickers bar.   On top of the can,
it sat still   on its back feet   tail lying limp

on the edge   like the Davy Crocket hat   on the closet
floor my son refuses   to wear,   its haunches undulating

big waves   with each breath,   no ribs visible, nothing taut
but the wrapper,   nothing urgent   nothing heard.

After Much Rain

". . . writhes above the water like visible light" Christian Wiman

Again, worms squirm on the driveway.
Last night's rain helps them believe
this wet slab of concrete will help
them breathe. But they are stuck,
writhing above a thin line of water.
Death is visible, and you pick up
one and toss it back in the grass,
any didactic metaphor lost on you,
and I've learned never to test
a kid on animal facts. Your empathy's
heart beats quicker now with each step
to worms driven here by last night's rain
with false hope—a joy they can't sustain.

Bodies in Chorus

a poem for my sons when they're told that sex is bad

What is there
between bodies in love
but devotion, selfless spirit,
a thread that pulls
together, announces, ordains,
seals the covenant gathered—
tangled, coupled
hearts, filled with tears
of joy of joy of joy
at the Father's creation.

Watching a Toddler
after Reading Christian Wiman

". . . before he's seized again with a sharp impersonal turbulence"

For Elise

What is the impersonal to you, not yet two, who points
in, toward, out of desire: the toy dinosaur, other people's

food, the stuffed animals on the couch, your dad, your mom,
the strangers milling about the room, the pacifier.

What is your index finger, this wand that summons
something out of nothing, that points and directs chaos

out of itself, beyond itself, to shape, to form a relation.
And these sounds? What are these incantations, sighs

too deep for grown-up understanding; they do not know
what to do or what they hear, but they obey, follow,

regardless, in spite of, or maybe to save, themselves?
What is the impersonal to you but slight turbulence

to be smoothed, each step forward, each object now
owned, possessed by a finger, no bigger than the empty

space where you now reside? And what are these blue
eyes, orbs that absorb the unfamiliar, the unknown,

as each of us wait by you, waiting to be chosen, to be made
known, your finger embedded in our longing but loosed grip?

Therefore

What is it there for, he often asked
the congregation. I know he meant

those words for Holy Scripture, but now
I keep looking behind me, to the left

and right of things, to see what I didn't see
before, to see what I forgot to see—

a sign, a path, a direction, a tiny point
on the blueprint of this life set here

before me. I think on it now: each book
to him, each fifty-cent find at the used

bookstore, each forgotten and abandoned
story on the library's free table becomes

a single word in a long sentence, always
pointing behind itself, like a pebble

in a stream, showing the subtle colored
marks and streaks, these bright veins—

a mineral's gift—from distant dirt,
the smoothness of the far-travelled water.

What is it there for, this clast cracked here
from its whole? What truth does it reveal?

After Watching *Wizard of Oz* with You

There's no place like home? But home is no place,
and place has no name, and name has no face,

but face is a hammer, and a hammer
needs a nail, and a nail craves a cross,

and a cross wants a body, and a body
is a body, and a body needs

a home, a place filled with names and faces
and always hammers and nails with crosses

in each room, and a body with a face
and a name above. Above? Yes, above

this face and body without the hammer
and the nails now is a home, a place

always here and not yet, but there are birds.
Birds now? Yes, of course. Don't we need love?

Notes

"On Their First Eucharist"
The Tolstoy reference comes from his short story "Master and Man" (1895).

"After They Are Criticized"
The reference comes from Henri J.M. Nouwen's book *Reaching Out: The Three Movements of the Spiritual Life* (Doubleday, 1975).

"When They Have a Difficult Time"
First, I use the Andrew George translation of the Epic of Gilgamesh (Penguin Book, 1999). Secondly, the form of this poem is influenced by Paige Lewis' "You Can Take Off Your Sweater, I've Made Today Warm" in the January 2108 issue of *Poetry.*

"Ash Wednesday"
"Uneasy lies the head that wears the crown" comes from Shakespeare's *King Henry the Fourth, Part Two.*

"For When My Sons Are Bored"
I refer to two poems here: Robert Frost's "Birches" and Robert Penn Warren's "Mortal Limit."

"When They Mow the Lawn"
I read this line in "A Conversation with Joy Kogawa" by Arthur Boers and Connie T. Braun in *Image Journal* Issue 95.

"The Juncos"
For Jacqueline Cannon Gable

"A Poem I Give to My Sons My Father Gave to Me"
This Latin phrase is translated differently, of course, but I am using a combination of "Where there is love, there is sight" and "Where there is love, there is insight" in this poem.

"The Painter"
The full quotation from Lennard J. Davis comes from his article "Constructing Normalcy: The Bell, Curve, the Novel and the Invention of the Disabled Body in the Nineteenth Century," found in *The Disability Studies Reader* (Routledge, NY 2006).

"Poverty"
This line from Nouwen also comes from his book *Reaching Out: The Three Movements of the Spiritual Life.*

"Joy Curves"
The Golden Shovel is a poetic form developed by Terrence Hayes in his poem "The Golden Shovel" in praise of Gwendolyn Brooks' famous poem "we real cool." In the form, the poet uses a line from another poem and places each word as the last word of the line in the new poem. I had the pleasure of learning about this form in a poetry workshop taught by Marilyn Nelson. My version uses a line from Nelson's poem "A Canticle for Abba Jacob," found in *Magnificat: Poems* (LSU Press, 1994).

"After Much Rain"
The line comes from Christian Wiman's "For D." in *Every Riven Thing* (FSG, 2011).

"Watching a Toddler"
The line comes from Christian Wiman's "Not Altogether Gone" in Every Riven Thing (FSG, 2011).

Acknowledgements

Jill Pelez Baumgaertner, poetry editor at *The Christian Century*, gave me the right amount encouragement to send a few of my poems to D.S. Martin, editor of the Poiema Poetry Series. This book would not exist without her affirmations and multiple kind gestures, nor would it exist without Don's careful and thoughtful editing.

Much of the writing and revising of these poems happened during a one-year sabbatical from my teaching and administrative duties at John Brown University, so I thank Chip Pollard and Ed Ericson for their continued support. As well, I thank the administration, faculty, and students at Handong Global University in Pohang, South Korea for welcoming me and providing me space to think and write during that year.

Several of my colleagues and friends were willing (or mostly so) to read poems and offer suggestions: Ben Egerton, Brad Gambill, Patty Kirk, Kinsley Koons Whitworth, and Jessica Hooten Wilson. I am very grateful for the thoughtful way they read these poems and cared for me. They're good people. Thank you to Eden Hinton for editing and formatting this book, while dealing with my anxiety and excitement.

Additionally, I am very grateful to the editors of the journals where many of the poems in this collection first appeared, although sometimes in very different versions: *Bird's Thumb*; *Cave Region Review*; *The Christian Century*; *Ekphrastic Review*; *Eunoia Review*; *Lullwater Review*; *Mobius: The Journal of Social Change*; *Nebo: A literary journal*; *Peacock Journal*; *The Penwood Review*; *Plough Quarterly*; *Presence*; *Rock and Sling*; *Whale Road Review*; *The Windhover*; and *Wordgathering*. Please consider supporting these journals with your patronage and your submissions.

Because I'm publishing my first book well into my 40s, I cannot help but think about every teacher who gave me good and bad advice; every friend who encouraged my writing; all of my family members, especially

ACKNOWLEDGEMENTS

my brother and parents, who choose to love me in all kinds of meaningful ways; and all of the people in my life who ever bought me a book or encouraged my reading; every book of poems; every setback and disappointment; every piece of writing advice, every workshop, every public reading, and every failed poem stuffed in a folder. I am very thankful for all of these experiences and for all of these people in my life, and I am grateful that you decided to read these poems.

Lastly, I am thankful for my wife Julia: her love, her level-headed encouragement, and for the one word she spoke after each acceptance and rejection: *Congratulations!* These poems are dedicated to our sons, which means, really, that they are dedicated to her.

The Poiema Poetry Series

COLLECTIONS IN THIS SERIES INCLUDE:

Six Sundays toward a Seventh by Sydney Lea

Epitaphs for the Journey by Paul Mariani

Within This Tree of Bones by Robert Siegel

Particular Scandals by Julie L. Moore

Gold by Barbara Crooker

A Word In My Mouth by Robert Cording

Say This Prayer into the Past by Paul Willis

Scape by Luci Shaw

Conspiracy of Light by D.S. Martin

Second Sky by Tania Runyan

Remembering Jesus by John Leax

What Cannot Be Fixed by Jill Pelaez Baumgaertner

Still Working It Out by Brad Davis

The Hatching of the Heart by Margo Swiss

Collage of Seoul by Jae Newman

Twisted Shapes of Light by William Jolliff

These Intricacies by David Harrity

Where the Sky Opens by Laurie Klein

True, False, None of the Above by Marjorie Maddox

The Turning Aside anthology edited by D.S. Martin

Falter by Marjorie Stelmach

Phases by Mischa Willett

Second Bloom by Anya Krugovoy Silver

Adam, Eve, & the Riders of the Apocalypse anthology edited by D.S. Martin

Your Twenty-First Century Prayer Life by Nathaniel Lee Hansen

Habitation of Wonder by Abigail Carroll

Ampersand by D.S. Martin

Full Worm Moon by Julie L. Moore

Ash & Embers by James A. Zoller

The Book of Kells by Barbara Crooker

Reaching Forever by Philip C. Kolin

The Book of Bearings by Diane Glancy

In a Strange Land anthology edited by D.S. Martin